Twenty to Make
Decorated Cup Cakes

Frances McNaughton

Search Press

First published in Great Britain 2009

Search Press Limited
Wellwood, North Farm Road,
Tunbridge Wells, Kent TN2 3DR

Reprinted 2010 (twice), 2011 (twice), 2013
Text copyright © Frances McNaughton 2009

Photographs by Roddy Paine Photographic Studios

Photographs and design copyright
© Search Press Ltd 2009

Print ISBN: 978-1-84448-519-2
Epub ISBN: 978-1-78126-022-7
Mobi ISBN: 978-1-78126-077-7
PDF ISBN: 978-1-78126-131-6

The Publishers and author can accept no
responsibility for any consequences arising from
the information, advice or instructions given in
this publication.

Suppliers
If you have difficulty in obtaining any of the
materials and equipment mentioned in this book,
then please visit the Search Press website for
details of suppliers: www.searchpress.com

Printed in Malaysia

*This book is dedicated to my sisters,
Annie, Rosie and Emma, and to my
brother, John.*

Contents

Introduction

Small is the new big! Cup cakes are a very
popular way of celebrating any special occasion.
They can be a colourful and tasty display for
any party table. Some modern weddings even
choose cup cakes as the centrepiece. Even if you
don't have a special occasion,
why not just make cakes for
family and friends – it's a great
way of practising
recipes and icing
ideas to use on
larger cakes.

There are many different cake recipes which can be used to make delicious cup cakes – in fact most cake recipes for large cakes are also suitable for making small cakes.

More and more people are discovering the delights of cake decorating by having a go at making cup cakes. I hope you have fun trying some of my ideas, and that having a go will spark a few ideas of your own.

Making cup cakes

This all-in-one sponge cake recipe makes twelve small cupcakes:

115g (4oz) self-raising flour, sieved
115g (4oz) soft cake margarine or soft butter
115g (4oz) caster sugar
2 eggs

1 Preheat the oven to 180°C/350°F/Gas mark 4. Line a cup cake tin with paper cases. Different tin sizes are available, and you can buy paper cases to go with each size.

2 Put all the ingredients in a bowl.

3 Beat with a wooden spoon for 2–3 minutes. If using a food mixer, reduce the beating time: only beat until the mixture becomes smooth and glossy.

4 Spoon the mixture into the cases – about half full for flatter cakes, about three-quarters full for more domed cakes.

5 Bake in the centre of the oven for 15–20 minutes until golden and the tops spring back when pressed gently. Allow longer baking time for deeper and larger cakes.

A large range of flat-iced cupcakes, plain fairy cakes and muffins are available in supermarkets and bakeries for those who just want to do the icing part! Small jelly sweets, melted chocolate, chocolate-covered stick biscuits, soft, golden sugar, edible glitter flakes and soft fudge have been used in this book to create simple designs.

Alternative flavours

Chocolate: add 15ml/1 tablespoon of cocoa powder mixed with 15ml/1 tablespoon of boiling water.

Lemon: add10ml/2 teaspoons of lemon juice and 5 ml/1 teaspoon of grated lemon rind.

Coffee: add 10ml/2 teaspoons of instant coffee dissolved in 5ml/1 teaspoon of hot water.

You can make different sizes from small sweet cases through to large muffin cases. Depending on the design you want to make, the cake can be baked so that it only fills up to the top of the case when baked, for a flat design; or it can be baked with more cake in the case, to form a dome when it is baked. If the cake rises more than you want, or is cracked on the surface, simply carve off the top to make it domed or flat.

Basic tools

Piping bags with piping tubes/nozzles

Small cutters in shapes such as primrose, small rose petal, holly leaf and heart

Round biscuit cutters (plain and frilly)

Quilt embosser

Cutting wheel

Flower centre tool

Small palette knife

Small rolling pin

Small, sharp scissors

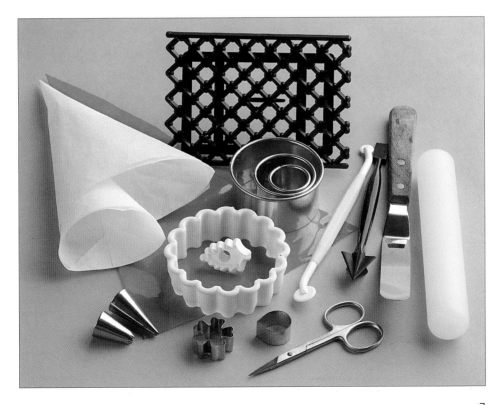

Over the Rainbow

Materials:

Cup cakes in brightly coloured cases

White frosting:

> 170g (6oz) white vegetable fat (shortening)
>
> 450g (16oz) icing sugar
>
> 3–4 tablespoons (45–60ml) milk or lemon juice
>
> Vanilla essence

Food colourings: blue, red, yellow and green

Tools:

Small palette knife

At least four greaseproof paper piping bags

No. 3 or 4 plain piping tube (or snip the end off a paper piping bag)

Instructions:

1 Make the white frosting by mixing the fat, sugar and flavouring, then beat in a few drops of water or milk to form a smooth, soft icing for piping. Using white vegetable fat keeps the icing white for the clouds, and blue for the sky. If you prefer to use butter for a better flavour, the clouds will look creamy and the blue will not be so bright.

2 Mix a portion of the frosting with red food colouring, another with yellow and another with green. Fill the piping bags (with or without the piping tubes) with a large spoonful each of frosting: white, red, yellow and green.

3 Mix blue colouring into the rest of the frosting and spread over the surface of each cake with a palette knife.

4 Pipe a curved red line half way round each cake, then repeat with the yellow, then the green.

5 Pipe little clouds at the ends of the rainbow.

Colourful rainbow cup cakes like these will brighten any party table.

Halloween Pumpkin

Materials:

Cup cakes baked in brightly coloured cases

Buttercream:

- 150g (6oz) butter
- 450g (16oz) icing sugar
- 3–4 tablespoons milk or lemon juice

Food colourings: egg yellow or orange; green

Dark chocolate, melted

Tools:

Small palette knife

Greaseproof paper piping bags

No. 2 plain piping tube

No. 4 plain piping tube (or snip the end off a paper piping bag)

Non-stick baking paper

Instructions:

1 Make the buttercream by mixing the butter and sugar, then beating in a few drops of milk or lemon juice to form a smooth, soft icing for piping.

2 Mix green colouring into a small portion of the buttercream and orange into the rest. Fill a small piping bag fitted with a No. 2 plain piping tube with a small spoonful of green buttercream. Fill a larger piping bag fitted with a No. 4 plain piping tube with orange-coloured buttercream.

3 Start the piping with a straight orange line down the centre, and then pipe either side, increasing the curve as each line is piped.

4 Pipe a few green lines at the top for leaves.

5 Put a small amount of melted dark chocolate into a small piping bag, and snip off a tiny piece of the end. You can then pipe a face directly on the cake. Alternatively, pipe it on to non-stick baking paper and leave it to set, then peel it off and stick it to the cake.

Make as many different scary pumpkin faces as you like for a Halloween party, or to hand out to trick or treaters.

Life's a Beach

Materials:

Cup cakes baked in brightly coloured cases

Fondant icing mix (not sugarpaste), available from sugarcraft shops and some supermarkets

Pink sugarpaste or modelling sugarpaste

Food colourings: blue and pink

Soft, golden caster sugar

Tools:

Small palette knife

Use the picture (right) to trace around the flip-flops to make a card template

Sharp knife or cutting wheel

Small rolling pin

Bowl

The templates for the flip-flops.

Instructions:

1 Using pink sugarpaste or modelling sugarpaste and the flip-flop templates, roll out and cut out the soles of the flip-flops. Cut out thin straps, dampen them with water and stick them on.

2 Mix the fondant icing, following the instructions on the packet. Gently warm to body temperature in a bowl over hot water, stirring occasionally. The fondant will be quite runny, but sets quite quickly as it cools.

3 Colour half of the fondant blue, and leave the other half white.

4 Spread blue fondant on half of each cake, and white on the other half.

5 Sprinkle the white half with soft, golden caster sugar, to look like sand.

6 Lay the flip-flops on top of each cake. If you want to make sure they are stuck on, spread a small dot of warmed fondant or buttercream under each heel , to act as glue.

Lazy Summer

For a variation, add a few drops of liquid green colour to desiccated coconut or granulated sugar, to look like grass. Dip half of the cup cake in the 'grass' to stick it on. Perfect for a summer party.

Beautiful Basket

Materials:

Cup cakes

Fondant icing mix (see page 12)

Chocolate buttercream:

> see the recipe on page 10, and add up to 30ml/ 2 tablespoons cocoa powder until you get the shade you like

Yellow sugarpaste for primroses

Tools:

Small palette knife

Greaseproof paper piping bags

Piping tube: small basketweave, rope or star

Small primrose flower cutter

Flower centre tool

Small rolling pin

Instructions:

1 Spread the fondant icing on top of each cake. This can be coloured if you prefer.

2 Fill a piping bag fitted with a basketweave, rope, or star piping tube with chocolate buttercream.

3 Start by piping the handle on top of each cake.

4 Then pipe a basket: start at one side, piping a vertical line, then pipe short lines across it, leaving the width of the piping tube between each line. Pipe a second vertical line, just covering the ends of the short horizontal lines. Pipe short lines across this second line, filling the gaps between the first and second vertical line. Pipe a third vertical line and continue piping short horizontal lines across. Continue across the cake until the basket is completed.

5 Roll out yellow sugarpaste and cut out primrose flowers. Stick on to the cup cake at the top of the basket by pushing the centre in with the flower centre tool.

14

Easter Egg Hunt

Make the basket in the same way, and add colourful jelly beans or tiny Easter eggs.

Fluffy Duck

Materials:

Cup cakes

Fondant icing (see page 12) coloured
with blue food colouring

Buttercream (see page 10) coloured
with yellow food colouring

Red or orange sugarpaste

Small amount of melted dark
chocolate for the eye

Tools:

Small palette knife

Piping bags

Large, plain piping tube

Instructions:

1 Spread the warmed blue fondant on each cake.

2 Fit the piping bag with the large, plain piping tube
and fill it with yellow buttercream.

3 Pipe a large ball for the head.

4 Pipe a large, fat curved teardrop for the body,
starting at the front. Pipe a smaller teardrop
for the wing, marking it with a palette knife
for the feathers.

5 Make a small beak from orange or
red sugarpaste and stick it into the
soft buttercream.

6 Pipe an eye with melted dark
chocolate in a piping bag.

Swanning Around

Make a swan in white frosting (see page 8 for recipe), starting with a long, curved head and neck. Pipe the dark beak and the eyes with chocolate.

Lionheart

Materials:

Cup cakes

Chocolate buttercream:

> See recipe on page 10, adding up to 30ml/ 2 tablespoons of cocoa powder until you get the shade you like

Sugarpaste coloured with autumn leaf colouring for the face. (Alternatively, use soft commercial fudge sweets. These can be warmed in the hands and moulded to shape)

Small amount of melted dark chocolate for the features

Tools:

Piping bags

Piping tube: basketweave, small rope or star

Small rolling pin

Heart cutter

Cocktail stick

Instructions:

1 Fill a piping bag fitted with a basketweave, rope, or star piping tube with chocolate buttercream.

2 Pipe wiggly lines starting at the centre and finishing with the point over the edge of the cake.

3 Mould coloured sugarpaste (or soft fudge) to form a heart shape. Use the picture as a guide, or roll out the paste and cut out using a heart-shaped cutter. Lay it on the cake.

4 Shape two small ovals for the cheeks. Press into place and mark with a cocktail stick.

5 Make two tiny balls of paste for the ears, flatten them slightly and pinch each base.

6 Pipe the eyes, nose and eyebrows with melted dark chocolate.

Tiger, Tiger

To make the tiger, use a plain piping tube and orange-coloured buttercream (see page 10) to pipe on to the cake. Shape the face in the same way as the lion using white sugarpaste. Pipe stripes, eyes, nose, and eyebrows with melted dark chocolate.

Checkmate

Materials:

Cup cakes with flat tops (cut the tops off
    if necessary)
225g (8oz) dark chocolate, melted
225g (8oz) white chocolate, melted

Tools:

Small palette knife
Piping bags
Non-stick baking paper

*The templates for
the chess pieces.*

Instructions:

1 Fill a small piping bag with melted dark
chocolate and another with melted
white chocolate.

2 Using the templates as a guide, pipe
out the chess pieces on to non-stick
baking paper. Set aside somewhere
cool, to harden.

3 Spread the top of each cake with
dark chocolate.

4 Pipe thin, straight lines across
each cake with white chocolate, then
pipe the other way to form a grid of
squares. Fill in alternate squares with
the melted white chocolate.

5 When the chess pieces are set, remove
carefully from the non-stick
paper and stick to each cake with a dot
of melted chocolate.

Dark Knight

Make a whole chess set and decorate each chess piece with chocolate in the opposite colour. If you prefer the taste of white chocolate, start each cake by spreading with white, instead of dark, chocolate. Perfect for the chess champion in your life.

Baby Blanket

Materials:

Cup cakes

Sugarpaste in blue or pink and white

Icing sugar for rolling out sugarpaste

Small amount of jam or buttercream, to stick the blanket to the cake

Tools:

Small rolling pin

Quilting embosser (or quilting can be marked on the sugarpaste using a knife with a ruler)

Tiny feet mould (alternatively, the feet can be modelled by hand from sugarpaste or piped using white frosting – recipe on page 8 – using the photograph as a guide)

Cutting wheel or knife

Square template made from card, slightly larger than the top of the cake

Opposite
Blue for a Boy
These delicate cup cakes are ideal for a baby shower or christening, or as a gift to celebrate a new arrival.

Instructions:

1 Roll out the sugarpaste in the colour of your choice, using icing sugar to stop it sticking to the work surface.

2 Emboss the surface of the icing to look like a quilted blanket.

3 Using your prepared template, cut the icing to form a square.

4 Spread a small amount of buttercream or jam on top of the cake and lay the icing blanket on top, with the points overhanging the edge.

5 Make tiny feet from white sugarpaste and stick on top of your cup cake.

Knitted Novelties

Materials:

At least seven cup cakes (can be domed or flat)

White frosting (see page 8)

Food colouring: I used yellow, green and blue to match the cases, but choose your own colours

Candy sticks from sweet shops

Small amount of white sugarpaste for the ends of the knitting needles

Tools:

Piping bags

Plain piping tube No. 3 or No. 4

Instructions:

1 Mix your chosen colours into the white frosting and place each in a piping bag fitted with a plain piping tube.

2 Pipe straight lines across each cake as shown, to look like loosely rolled balls of wool.

3 Pipe a spiral line down one of the candy sticks and push the end of the stick into one of the cup cakes.

4 Continue piping loops in rows along the stick to look like knitting.

5 Push the other candy stick into the same cup cake.

6 Dampen the top ends of the candy sticks and press a small flattened ball of sugarpaste on to each one.

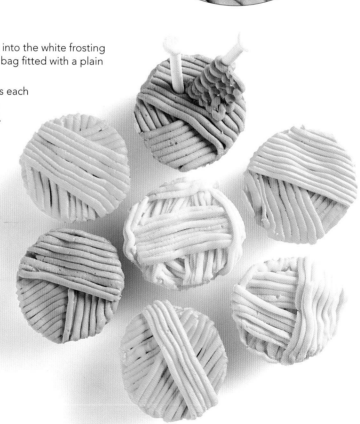

This colourful collection of cup cakes would be ideal for celebrating the birthday of a friend who loves knitting.

Daisy, Daisy

Materials:

At least nine flat-topped cup cakes

White frosting (see page 8)

Food colouring: yellow for the flower centre
and green for leaves

Tools:

Small palette knife

Piping bags

Large, plain piping tube

Instructions:

1 Mix yellow food colouring with some of the frosting and green with another portion, and leave the rest white. Spread the white frosting over the top of six of the cakes.

2 Pipe large petals across each cake using a plain piping tube.

3 Pipe a large yellow swirl on top of one cake using a large, plain piping tube.

4 Spread green frosting over two cakes.

5 Pipe large green leaves (shown on opposite page) using a plain or a leaf piping tube.

Celebrate a keen gardener, or a friend named Daisy, with this crazy daisy cup cake display.

Spanish Fan

Materials:

Cup cakes baked in red cases
Buttercream (see page 10 for recipe)
Red food colouring
Food colouring powders: red and edible gold
Edible painting solution/alcohol
Sugar modelling paste

Tools:

Small palette knife
Piping bags
Piping tube: star or rope

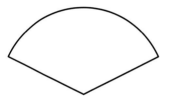

Instructions:

1 Make fans by rolling out thin sugar modelling paste using the template. Mark lines on the fans with a palette knife.

2 Paint the fans with red powder food colouring and edible gold powder, each mixed with painting solution/ alcohol. Leave the fans to dry, preferably overnight, turning occasionally.

3 Spread the tops of the cup cakes with red buttercream.

4 Pipe around the edge of each cake using a star or rope tube.

5 Push the dry fans into the tops of the cup cakes.

This fantastic cup cake has a Spanish look, but you could change the colours to create an oriental theme.

Strawberry Cream

Materials:

Cup cakes: as a variation, you could put a single strawberry in each case before you put the cake batter in – it will then cook inside the cake

White chocolate ganache: 1 part double cream to 3 parts white chocolate; e.g.

    150g (6oz) double cream

    450g (18oz) white chocolate

Fresh strawberries

Tools:

Piping bags

Piping tube: large star or rope

Instructions:

1 Melt the white chocolate. Bring the double cream to the boil and immediately turn off the heat. Mix together. Leave to cool in a fridge until thick enough to pipe with. If the ganache is too stiff, allow it to come back to room temperature, or beat it in a food mixer, adding a little more double cream to help soften it.

2 Pipe a large swirl of white chocolate ganache on top of each cup cake, starting from the outside edge and coming up to a point in the middle.

3 Decorate with a fresh strawberry.

Opposite
Raspberry Reverie
For a delicious dark chocolate alternative, use chocolate cake instead of vanilla, and put a raspberry in the bottom of the cake before it is cooked. Dark chocolate ganache is made with equal parts of chocolate to buttercream; e.g. 300g (12oz) double cream to 300g (12oz) dark chocolate.

Ice Cream Dream

Materials:

Flat-bottomed ice cream cones
Crispy rice breakfast cereal
100g (3½oz) white chocolate, melted
Buttercream (see page 10)
Ice cream sauce, fruit flavour

Tools:

Piping bag
Piping tube: large star or rope

Instructions:

1 Mix melted white chocolate with the crispy rice cereal – enough to coat each grain to make them stick together. Fill each of the ice cream cones to a dome on top (see above). Leave to cool.

2 Pipe a large swirl of buttercream, starting from the outside edge and coming up to a point in the middle.

3 Drizzle the top with fruit flavour ice cream sauce.

Opposite

These ice cream dreams are a departure from traditional cup cakes, with chocolate-covered crispy rice cake as the base. You could make your own fruit purée or melt chocolate to drizzle over the top, then sprinkle with tiny sweets or chopped nuts.

Flowerpot

Materials:
Chocolate cup cakes, domed on top

Chocolate-covered stick biscuits or chocolate sticks

Small jelly sweets

White chocolate, melted

Tools:
Small piping bags

Non-stick baking paper

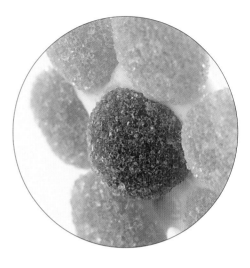

Instructions:

1 Pipe a small blob of melted white chocolate on to non-stick baking paper. Lay the end of a chocolate-covered stick biscuit or chocolate stick into the chocolate. Leave to cool and set (this can be speeded up by putting the stick and chocolate in the refrigerator).

2 When set, pipe another small blob of chocolate on top of the first one, and stick in coloured jelly sweets to form a flower. Attach a couple of green jelly sweets lower down the stick, using melted chocolate. Leave to cool and set.

3 Push the chocolate stick stem into the top of the cup cake.

Opposite
These potty cup cakes make a lovely alternative to a pot plant as a gift, or they will be a real hit at children's parties.

34

Wedding Cake

Materials:

Cup cakes baked in silver cases, flat-topped

Cup cakes baked in tiny silver sweet cases

Fondant icing (see page 12)

Sugar modelling paste/ flower paste

Small amount of green buttercream

Tools:

Small rolling pin

Small rose petal cutter

Piping bags

Palette knife

Instructions:

1 To make an arum lily, roll out sugar modelling paste or flower paste thinly. Cut out small rose petals with the rose petal cutter. Roll each one between your fingers to form a spiral with the point of the petal at the top. Leave to one side to set.

2 Spread warmed white fondant icing over each cake, placing the tiny cake on top of the larger one straight away so that it will stick.

3 Pipe small green stems and long leaves on the cakes and press the flowers into place.

These beautiful cakes could also be served for wedding anniversary celebrations, made in different coloured cases. As an alternative, make the cakes in gold cases, and colour the fondant icing to a soft ivory.

White Christmas

Materials:

Cup cakes

Fondant icing (see page 12)

White or green sugarpaste
    for the trees

Edible sparkles

Tools:

Sharp, pointed scissors

Piping bags

Palette knife

Instructions:

1 Make a solid, pointed cone shape from around 20g (¾oz) sugarpaste. Starting at the point of the cone, snip tiny 'v' shapes with sharp, pointed scissors, close to the surface of the paste, working round and down to look like a simple fir tree. Cut off the bottom of the cone when you get to the size of tree you would like.

2 Spread the top of each cake with warmed fondant. Stick the prepared tree on to the top of the cake while the fondant is still soft.

3 Sprinkle the tree and cake with edible sparkles.

Snow Drift

For another spectacular Christmas treat, bake the cake in a gold case and make the tree in white sugarpaste. Pipe a garland of fondant around the tree using a piping bag with the end cut off.

Ladybird

Materials:

Cup cakes with domed tops (carved to form a smooth dome)

Red sugarpaste

Black sugarpaste

Small piece of white sugarpaste for the eyes

Buttercream or jam for sticking the icing to the cake

Icing sugar for rolling out paste

Tools:

Small rolling pin

Palette knife

Small circle cutters

Instructions:

1 Make a circle template large enough to cover the whole of the dome of the cake. You might find a bowl or saucer in the kitchen to use as a template.

2 Spread a little buttercream or jam on each cup cake ready to stick on the sugarpaste.

3 Roll out the red sugarpaste and cut out using the circle template. Lay the paste on the cake and smooth it out evenly. Mark a line across the middle with the palette knife for the wings.

4 Roll out black sugarpaste, cut out a smaller circle, dampen it slightly with water and stick it on to the edge to the cake for the face. Cut off the excess to the edge of the red paste.

5 Use the edge of a small circle cutter to press in a smiling mouth.

6 Eyes and spots on the back can be cut out using small circle cutters, or moulded by hand. Make two small circles of white sugarpaste and stick on to the face. Make two smaller black circles, and stick them on top of the white. Two larger circles of black stuck on to the back make the ladybird's spots.

What a Buzz!

Cover the cake with a large circle of black sugarpaste. Make the face in the same way as the ladybird. Cut out strips of yellow sugarpaste and stick on to the black. Wings can be made by cutting oval shapes from rice paper. Make incisions in the paste where the wings will go, and push the ends of the wings in.

Family Tree

Materials:

Work out how many cup cakes you need for your family tree

Buttercream (see page 10)

Chocolate buttercream; add up to 30ml/ 2 tablespoons cocoa powder to buttercream until you get the shade you like

Flesh-coloured sugarpaste: I used paprika food colouring, but different skin colours can be made by using different strengths or mixing shades of autumn leaf, paprika, chestnut and dark brown

Black food colouring for the eyes

Food colouring for hair, and green for leaves

Tools:

Palette knife

Piping bags

Piping tubes: plain no. 2 and leaf

Cocktail stick

Drinking straw – cut the end off at a slight angle for marking smiling mouths

Instructions:

1 Model flesh-coloured sugarpaste into oval and round shapes for simple faces. Mark a smile on each with the end of a drinking straw.

2 Make tiny noses and stick them on. You could also make ears, if they are in character.

3 Spread chocolate buttercream on each of the cakes, and gently press the faces into place.

4 Mark the eyes by dipping the end of a cocktail stick into black food colouring, then pushing it into each face.

5 Pipe the name on each cake with buttercream.

6 Mix up small amounts of buttercream with food colouring for the hair and pipe the hair on for each character.

7 Mix buttercream with green food colouring. With a leaf tube in a piping bag, pipe green leaves over the rest of each cake.

This collection of cup cakes would be a lovely surprise for a family reunion, a grandparent's birthday, or to mark a new arrival in the family. Leaves could be made from sugarpaste cut out with different leaf cutters, rather than piping. Instead of a family tree, you could make named cakes for children coming to a birthday party.

Engagement Ring

Materials:

Cup cakes baked in gold cases
Fondant icing (see page 12)
Chocolate stick biscuits
Small amount of sugarpaste for the ring
Colourless firm jelly sweets
Edible sparkles
Gold powder food colouring
Alcohol for painting

Tools:

Extra gold cake cases for the lids
Palette knife
Sharp, pointed scissors

Instructions:

1 Spread each cake with warmed fondant icing. Push two chocolate stick biscuits into the cake to support the 'lid'.

2 Make a short thin sausage of sugarpaste and stick on the top of the cake to look like the ring. Make a slight dip in the middle to hold the 'diamond'. Paint with gold food colouring.

3 With sharp, pointed scissors, cut a colourless firm jelly sweet to a rough diamond shape. For added shine, roll the 'diamond' in edible sparkles. Stick it on to the ring by dampening slightly with water (not wet).

4 Put a small amount of warmed fondant in the empty cake case. When it has cooled and set (should only take a few minutes) turn the case over and push the chocolate sticks gently into the fondant, to form the lid.

44

A tasty and romantic treat for an engagement party! Different coloured jelly sweets could be used to create a variety of precious stones.

Shamrock

Materials:
Cup cakes

Orange sugarpaste

Green sugarpaste

Small amount of buttercream or jam

Icing sugar

Tools:
Wavy-edged round cookie cutter,
   slightly bigger than your cake

Heart cutter

Palette knife

Rolling pin

Instructions:
1 Spread a little jam or buttercream on each cake.

2 Roll out the orange sugarpaste, with a little icing sugar to stop it sticking to the surface.

3 Cut out the sugarpaste with the large cutter and lay the icing over the cake. Smooth it with your hand.

4 Roll out the green sugarpaste and cut out three heart shapes for each shamrock. Lay them straight on to the cake as shown. If they need to be stuck on, dampen under each heart slightly with water.

5 Make a small green stem from the sugarpaste.

Sweet Thistle

Use purple sugarpaste for the top of the cake. Stick on a small flattened ball of purple sugarpaste and mark with a knife as shown. Roll out green sugarpaste and cut out two holly leaves with a cutter and the central shape by hand. Attach the central shape under the purple strands. Mark with 'v' shapes. Stick the two holly leaves underneath and mark the leaves with a knife.

You are invited to visit the
author's website
www.franklysweet.co.uk

Publishers' Note
If you would like more information
about sugarcraft, try *Sugar Animals*
by Frances McNaughton,
Search Press, 2009.

Acknowledgements
Special thanks to the team at
Search Press for all their hard work:
editor Sophie Kersey, designer Marrianne
Mercer and photographer Gavin Sawyer
at Roddy Paine Photographic Studios.
Also to Mike for his continuing support
and encouragement.